New Jersey Post Office Mural Guidebook

David W. Gates Jr.

POST OFFICE FANS
Crystal Lake, Illinois

Copyright © 2021 David W. Gates Jr.
1st Edition

New Jersey Post Office Mural Guidebook / David W. Gates Jr.

ISBN: 978-1-970088-15-1 (Paperback)
ISBN: 978-1-970088-16-8 (EPUB)
ISBN: 978-1-970088-17-5 (PDF)

All rights reserved. No part of this publication may be reproduced, stored, or transmitted in any form or by any means, electronic, mechanical, photocopying, recording, scanning, or otherwise, without written permission from the publisher. It is illegal to copy this book, post it to a website, or distribute it by any other means without permission.

David W. Gates Jr. asserts the moral right to be identified as the author of this work.

Neither David W. Gates Jr. nor the publisher are responsible for the persistence or accuracy of URLs for external or third-party internet websites referred to in this publication and do not guarantee that any content on such websites is, or will remain, accurate or appropriate.

Designations used by companies to distinguish their products are often claimed as trademarks. All brand names and product names used in this book and on its cover are trade names, service marks, trademarks and registered trademarks of their respective owners. Neither the book nor the publishers are associated with any product or vendor mentioned in this book. None of the companies referenced within the book have endorsed the book.

To contact the publisher:

Post Office Fans
PO Box 11
Crystal Lake, IL 60039
Phone: 815-206-8405
info@postofficefans.com • www.postofficefans.com

Cover and text design by John Reinhardt Book Design
Front cover photo: Bordentown Post Office, Bordentown, New Jersey

Contents

Preface vii
Introduction 1

Atlantic City 3
Boonton 4
Bordentown 5
Caldwell 6
Cliffside Park 7
Clifton 8
Cranford 9
Fort Lee 10
Freehold 11
Garfield 12
Glen Ridge 13
Gloucester City 14
Haddon Heights 15
Hammonton 16
Harrison 17
Hawthorne 18
Kearny 19
Linden 20
Little Falls 21
Matawan 22
Metuchen 23
Millburn 24

Mount Holly 25
New Brunswick 26
New Brunswick (Cont'd) 27
Newark Post Office & Courthouse 28
Newark Post Office & Courthouse (Cont'd) 29
North Bergen 30
Nutley 31
Paulsboro 32
Penns Grove 33
Pitman 34
Plainfield 35
Pompton Lakes 36
Princeton 37
Ridgefield Park 38
Ridgewood 39
Riverside 40
Short Hills 41
South Orange 42
South River 43
Summit 44
Toms River 45
Trenton 46
Washington 47
West New York 48
Westfield 49
Westwood 50
Wildwood 51

Summary 53
About the Author 55
Other Titles by the Publisher 57

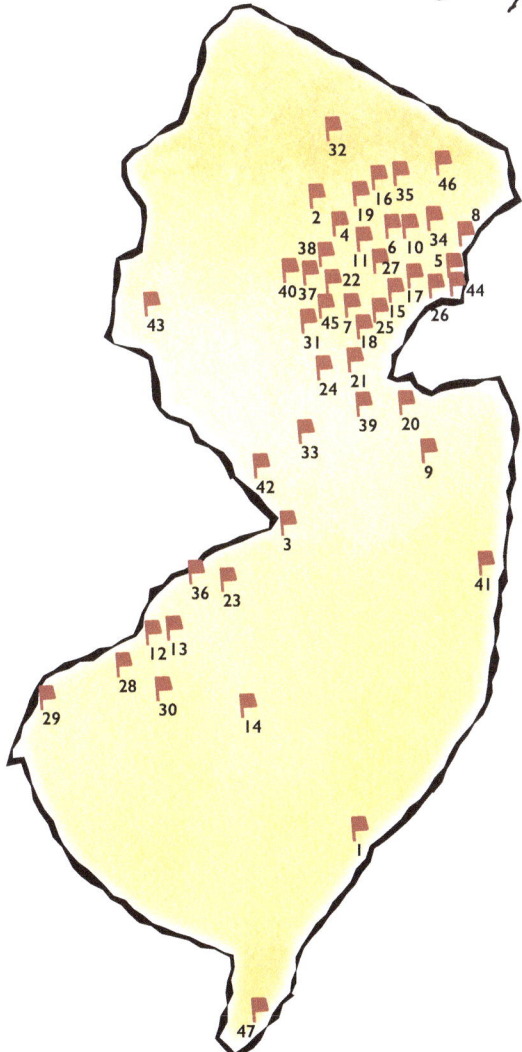

New Jersey Post Office Murals

1. Atlantic City
2. Boonton
3. Bordentown
4. Caldwell
5. Cliffside Park
6. Clifton (former)
7. Cranford
8. Fort Lee
9. Freehold (former)
10. Garfield
11. Glen Ridge
12. Gloucester City
13. Haddon Heights
14. Hammonton
15. Harrison
16. Hawthorne
17. Kearny
18. Linden
19. Little Falls (former)
20. Matawan
21. Metuchen
22. Millburn
23. Mount Holly
24. New Brunswick
25. Newark
26. North Bergen
27. Nutley
28. Paulsboro
29. Penns Grove
30. Pitman
31. Plainfield
32. Pompton Lakes
33. Princeton (former)
34. Ridgefield Park
35. Ridgewood
36. Riverside
37. Short Hills
38. South Orange
39. South River
40. Summit
41. Toms River (former)
42. Trenton (former)
43. Washington
44. West New York
45. Westfield
46. Westwood
47. Wildwood

Preface

THE STATISTICS I'VE READ report there are somewhere between 1,100 and 1,400 works of art located in public post offices nationwide. Since I've been unable to verify these statistics, I've made it my mission to find out exactly how many exist and to view them all.

What began for me as a casual interest in a photographic subject soon became a deep fascination with the history and presence of a unique moment in American culture and art. Before creating this guidebook, I visited hundreds of post offices and spoke to dozens of people across the U.S., and I realized we were united in our enthusiasm for keeping the stories of this art alive and available for the American public.

The guidebook you are viewing today is an account of all 47 of New Jersey's New Deal post office murals. I encourage you to visit one of these post offices in New Jersey or seek out one in your own state. To learn about this special art is to learn about the continuing American journey.

Our guidebooks continue to be a great resource for post office enthusiasts. The potential fate of the Fort Lee building drove me to accelerate plans for writing the New Jersey guidebook. It is my goal to show how important it is to keep this history alive. This book provides a quick reference to the Depression-era murals in New Jersey.

There are no images of the murals in this book. It is meant solely as a reference to the buildings and towns. This guide provides: full address, title of the artwork, artist, medium, and status. I've found having a book like this makes for a handy reference and personal checklist while traveling around the state.

I've created this guidebook for your benefit, in case you find yourself needing the same checklist as you travel and discover each building and mural. I hope this book brings you enjoyment and knowledge. There is no need to scour multiple sources to find the status of each one. I've done the work for you. Print it out or download it to your mobile device to bring with you on your next post office visit.

Thank you,

David W. Gates Jr.

Introduction

FROM 1934–1943, fascinating murals and various forms of art were commissioned and installed in public buildings under the United States Treasury Department's Section of Painting and Sculpture, later renamed the Section of Fine Arts.

My research revealed two reasons for installing art in post offices. The first was to bring light and hope to a country gripped by the Great Depression, and the second was to employ artists during this difficult time.

Anonymous competitions were held to select artists for new federal buildings that were being constructed during this time. Commissions paid to the artists were approximately one percent of the congressional appropriation to construct the new post office buildings.

This informative book lists all the post offices in New Jersey that received artwork. It gives you a quick reference to the New Deal post office murals in New Jersey. It includes:

- Full address
- Artist
- Title
- Medium
- Status
- Link for further reading

While this guide does not provide images of the art, it does provide a quick reference to the post office art in New Jersey. Although the title of the book says "mural," I use that term inclusively. New Jersey is lucky to have also receive art commissioned in other mediums such as wood, plaster, terra-cotta, stone, and bronze.

Atlantic City

ADDRESS: 801 Atlantic Ave., Ste. 101, Atlantic City, New Jersey 08401

ARTIST: Peppino Mangravite

TITLE: *Family Recreations* and *Youth*

MEDIUM: Oil on canvas (murals) 2 panels

STATUS: The former historic Atlantic City post office was razed. The murals were moved to the new building shown here. The murals reside behind glass cases in the main lobby of the building. They can be viewed by interested members of the public during business hours.

WEB: https://www.postofficefans.com/atlantic-city-new-jersey-post-office/

Boonton

ADDRESS: 501 Main St., Boonton, New Jersey 07005

ARTIST: Enid Bell

TITLE: *Morning Mail*

MEDIUM: Wood (relief)

STATUS: The former Boonton post office was razed. The relief was moved to the newer building shown here. It can be viewed by interested members of the public. It resides on the wall in the retail section of the main lobby. It is only viewable during business hours.

WEB: https://www.postofficefans.com/boonton-new-jersey-post-office/

Bordentown

ADDRESS: 14 Walnut St., Bordentown, New Jersey 08505

ARTIST: Avery Johnson

TITLE: *Skating on Bonaparte's Pond*

MEDIUM: Oil on canvas (mural)

STATUS: The Bordentown post office is still an active, operating facility, and the mural can be viewed by interested members of the public. It resides in the lobby on the wall above the postmaster's door. The Bordentown mural was the winner in the 48 States mural competition in 1939.

WEB: https://www.postofficefans.com/bordentown-new-jersey-post-office/

CALDWELL

ADDRESS: 10 Park Ave., Caldwell, New Jersey 07006

ARTIST: Brenda Putnam

TITLE: *Sorting the Mail*

MEDIUM: Plaster (lunette)

STATUS: The Caldwell post office is still an active, operating facility. However, the lunette was removed from this facility, and placed in the newer building on Clinton Road. It formerly resided in the lobby on the wall above the postmaster's door. As of this writing, the art is covered up and not viewable until a future dedication. It resides on a wall in the main lobby above the post office boxes.

WEB: https://www.postofficefans.com/caldwell-new-jersey-post-office/

Cliffside Park

ADDRESS: 289 Gorge Rd., Cliffside Park, New Jersey 07010

ARTIST: Bruno Neri

TITLE: *Rural Delivery*

MEDIUM: Plaster (relief)

STATUS: The former historic Cliffside Park post office constructed in 1935 was razed in early 2000. The relief once housed in the building has been reported missing, lost, or destroyed. It originally resided in the lobby above the postmaster's door.

WEB: https://www.postofficefans.com/former-cliffside-park-new-jersey-post-office/

CLIFTON

ADDRESS: 1232 Main Ave., Clifton, New Jersey 07011

ARTIST: John Sitton

TITLE: *Transportation*

MEDIUM: Oil on canvas (mural) 6 panels

STATUS: The former Clifton post office shown here is no longer an active postal facility. Unfortunately, the panels are reported missing, lost, or destroyed. It is not clear if they were painted over or removed. They formerly resided in the rotunda, on the walls of what was once the main entrance. Newer sports murals are currently in the spaces where the original murals would have been located. Interested members of the public should contact the Clifton recreation center for current hours and accessibility.

WEB: https://www.postofficefans.com/former-clifton-new-jersey-post-office/

CRANFORD

ADDRESS: 3 Miln St., Cranford, New Jersey 07016

ARTIST: Gerald Foster

TITLE: *The Battle of Cranford during the American Revolution*

MEDIUM: Oil on canvas (murals) 3 panels

STATUS: The Cranford post office is still an active, operating facility, and the murals can be viewed by interested members of the public. One large panel resides on a wall in the main lobby. A second panel resides on an adjacent wall above the mailboxes. One smaller panel resides in the retail section of the lobby.

WEB: https://www.postofficefans.com/cranford-new-jersey-post-office/

FORT LEE

ADDRESS: 229 Main St., Fort Lee, New Jersey 07024

ARTIST: Henry Schnakenberg

TITLE: *Indians Trading with the Half Moon, Washington at Fort Lee, Moving Pictures at Fort Lee,* and *The Present Day*

MEDIUM: Oil on canvas (murals) 4 panels

STATUS: The Fort Lee post office is still an active, operating facility, and the murals can be viewed by interested members of the public. Three reside on the wall of the main lobby above the retail counter and one resides above the postmaster's door. At the time of this publication, the borough has plans to demolish the building and the murals are slated to be relocated to the community center.

WEB: https://www.postofficefans.com/fort-lee-new-jersey-post-office/

FREEHOLD

ADDRESS: 50 E. Main St., Freehold, New Jersey 07728

ARTIST: Gerald Foster

TITLE: *Molly Pitcher*

MEDIUM: Tempera (mural)

STATUS: The former Freehold post office shown here is no longer an active, operating facility. It is home to the Monmouth County Health Department. The mural that once resided here was moved to the Monmouth County public library. It can be viewed by interested members of the public during library hours.

WEB: https://www.postofficefans.com/former-freehold-new-jersey-post-office/

Garfield

ADDRESS: 254 Palisade Ave., Garfield, New Jersey 07026

ARTIST: Robert Laurent

TITLE: *Transportation of the Mail*

MEDIUM: Stone (sculpture)

STATUS: The Garfield post office is still an active, operating facility. The sculpture can be viewed by interested members of the public. It resides in the lobby on the wall above the postmaster's door.

WEB: https://www.postofficefans.com/garfield-new-jersey-post-office

Glen Ridge

ADDRESS: 225 Ridgewood Ave., Glen Ridge, New Jersey 07028

ARTIST: James Chapin

TITLE: *Glen Ridge*

MEDIUM: Oil on canvas (mural)

STATUS: The Glen Ridge post office is still an active, operating facility, and the mural can be viewed by interested members of the public. It resides in the lobby on the wall above the postmaster's door.

WEB: https://www.postofficefans.com/glen-ridge-new-jersey-post-office

GLOUCESTER CITY

ADDRESS: 113 Broadway, Gloucester City, New Jersey 08030

ARTIST: Vincent D'Agostino

TITLE: *The Perils of the Mail*

MEDIUM: Oil on canvas (mural)

STATUS: The Gloucester City post office is still an active, operating facility. The mural can be viewed by interested members of the public. It resides in the lobby on the wall above the postmaster's door.

WEB: https://www.postofficefans.com/gloucester-city-new-jersey-post-office/

Haddon Heights

ADDRESS: 701 Station Ave., Haddon Heights, New Jersey 08035

ARTIST: Isamu Noguchi

TITLE: *The Letter*

MEDIUM: Stone (relief)

STATUS: The Haddon Heights post office is still an active, operating facility, and the relief can be viewed by interested members of the public. It resides in the lobby on the wall above the postmaster's door.

WEB: https://www.postofficefans.com/haddon-heights-new-jersey-post-office

Hammonton

ADDRESS: 114 S. 3rd St., Hammonton, New Jersey 08037

ARTIST: Spero Anargyros

TITLE: *Harvest*

MEDIUM: Stone (sculpture)

STATUS: The Hammonton post office is still an active, operating facility. However, the sculpture has been reported missing, lost, or destroyed. It was previously located in the lobby above the postmaster's door.

WEB: https://www.postofficefans.com/hammonton-new-jersey-post-office/

Harrison

ADDRESS: 427 Harrison Ave., Harrison, New Jersey 07029

ARTIST: Murray J. Roper

TITLE: *Industry and the Family*

MEDIUM: Plaster (relief)

STATUS: The Harrison post office is still an active, operating facility, and the relief can be viewed by interested members of the public. It resides in the lobby on the wall above the postmaster's door.

WEB: https://www.postofficefans.com/harrison-new-jersey-post-office/

Hawthorne

ADDRESS: 226 Diamond Bridge Ave., Hawthorne, New Jersey 07506

ARTIST: Ilse Erythropel

TITLE: *Postman and Hawthorne Bush*

MEDIUM: Wood (relief)

STATUS: The Hawthorne post office is still an active, operating facility and the relief can be viewed by interested members of the public. It resides in the lobby on the wall above the post office boxes.

WEB: https://www.postofficefans.com/hawthorne-new-jersey-post-office/

Kearny

ADDRESS: 64 Midland Ave., Kearny, New Jersey 07032

ARTIST: Albert Kotin

TITLE: *The City* and *The Marsh*

MEDIUM: Oil on canvas (murals) 2 panels

STATUS: The Kearny post office is still an active, operating facility, and the murals can be viewed by interested members of the public. One mural resides in the main lobby on the wall above the bulletin boards. The other resides in the retail section of the lobby above the postmaster's door.

WEB: https://www.postofficefans.com/kearny-new-jersey-post-office/

LINDEN

ADDRESS: 400 N. Wood Ave., Ste. A, Linden, New Jersey 07036

ARTIST: Sahl Swarz

TITLE: *Industry*

MEDIUM: Terra-cotta (relief)

STATUS: The Linden post office is still an active, operating facility, and the relief can be viewed by interested members of the public. It resides in the lobby on the wall above the postmaster's door.

WEB: https://www.postofficefans.com/linden-new-jersey-post-office/

Little Falls

ADDRESS: 19 Warren St., Little Falls, New Jersey 07424

ARTIST: James Brooks

TITLE: *Labor and Leisure*

MEDIUM: Oil on canvas (mural)

STATUS: The former Little Falls post office is no longer an active, operating facility. However, the mural still resides in the building. Interested members of the public should contact the civic center for current hours and accessibility. The mural resides in the lobby on the wall above what was once the postmaster's door.

WEB: https://www.postofficefans.com/former-little-falls-new-jersey-post-office/

Matawan

ADDRESS: 155 Main St., Matawan, New Jersey 07747

ARTIST: Armin Alfred Scheler

TITLE: *Philip Freneau Freeing the Slaves, Rural Mail, Old Hospital, Old Glenwood Institute*, and *First Presbyterian Church, 1767*

MEDIUM: Plaster (reliefs) 5 individual reliefs

STATUS: The Matawan post office is still an active, operating facility, and the reliefs can be viewed by interested members of the public. Four of them reside on the walls of the main lobby, brilliantly showcased by modern motion sensor lighting for your enjoyment. The fifth one resides in the retail section of the lobby, accessible only during business hours.

WEB: https://www.postofficefans.com/matawan-new-jersey-post-office/

Metuchen

ADDRESS: 360 Main St., Metuchen, New Jersey 08840

ARTIST: Harold Ambellan

TITLE: *Gardeners*

MEDIUM: Plaster (relief)

STATUS: The Metuchen post office is still an active, operating facility, and the relief can be viewed by interested members of the public. It resides on the wall in the main lobby above the postmaster's door.

WEB: https://www.postofficefans.com/metuchen-new-jersey-post-office/

Millburn

ADDRESS: 300 Millburn Ave., Millburn, New Jersey 07041

ARTIST: Gerald Foster

TITLE: *Revolutionary Engagement at Bridge in Millburn—1780*

MEDIUM: Oil on canvas (mural)

STATUS: The Millburn post office is still an active, operating facility. However, the mural is reported to be missing, lost, or destroyed. It formerly resided on the wall in the main lobby above the postmaster's door.

WEB: https://www.postofficefans.com/millburn-new-jersey-post-office/

Mount Holly

ADDRESS: 28 Washington St., Mt. Holly, New Jersey 08060

ARTIST: Enid Bell

TITLE: *The Post—1790*

MEDIUM: Wood (relief)

STATUS: The Mount Holly post office is still an active, operating facility, and the relief can be viewed by interested members of the public. It resides in the lobby on the wall above the postmaster's door.

WEB: https://www.postofficefans.com/mount-holly-new-jersey-post-office/

New Brunswick

ADDRESS: 86 Bayard St., New Brunswick, New Jersey 08901

ARTIST: George Biddle

TITLE: *George Washington with De Witt, Geographer of the Revolutionary Army/Washington Retreating from New Brunswick*; and *Howe and Cornwallis Entering New Brunswick*

MEDIUM: Oil on canvas (murals) 2 panels

STATUS: The New Brunswick post office is still an active, operating facility, and the murals can be viewed by interested members of the public. They reside on the walls of the vestibule.

WEB: https://www.postofficefans.com/new-brunswick-new-jersey-post-office/

New Brunswick

(CONT'D)

ADDRESS: 86 Bayard St., New Brunswick, New Jersey 08901

ARTIST: Ruth Nickerson

TITLE: *The Dispatch Rider*

MEDIUM: Unknown (sculpture)

STATUS: The New Brunswick post office is still an active, operating facility. Unfortunately, the sculpture has been reported missing, lost, or destroyed. Multiple attempts to determine the fate of this one have not been successful. However, there is one known image of the art in the National Archives records.

WEB: https://www.postofficefans.com/new-brunswick-new-jersey-post-office/

Newark Post Office & Courthouse

ADDRESS: 2 Federal Square, Newark, New Jersey 07102

ARTIST: Romuald Kraus

TITLE: *Justice*

MEDIUM: Bronze (sculpture)

STATUS: The Newark Post Office and Courthouse is still an active, operating facility. However, the statue is not easily accessible. Interested members of the public have been directed to get written approval from the judge or have official court business to view the art. It resides on the third floor of the building where the courtrooms are located.

WEB: https://www.postofficefans.com/newark-new-jersey-post-office/

Newark Post Office & Courthouse (cont'd)

ADDRESS: 2 Federal Square, Newark, New Jersey 07102

ARTIST: Vicken von Post Totten

TITLE: *Two medallions representing light and darkness*

MEDIUM: Metal (medallions)

STATUS: The Newark Post Office and Courthouse is still an active, operating facility. However, the whereabouts of these two medallions are currently unknown. At the time of this publication, they are reported missing, lost, or destroyed.

WEB: https://www.postofficefans.com/newark-new-jersey-post-office/

North Bergen

ADDRESS: 4608 Tonnelle Ave., North Bergen, New Jersey 07047

ARTIST: Avery Johnson

TITLE: *Purchase of Territory of North Bergen from the Indians*

MEDIUM: Oil on canvas (mural)

STATUS: The North Bergen post office is still an active, operating facility, and the mural can be viewed by interested members of the public. It resides in the lobby on the wall above the postmaster's door.

WEB: https://www.postofficefans.com/north-bergen-new-jersey-post-office/

Nutley

ADDRESS: 372 Franklin Ave., Nutley, New Jersey 07110

ARTIST: Paul C. Chapman

TITLE: *Return of Annie Oakley*

MEDIUM: Oil on canvas (mural)

STATUS: The Nutley post office is still an active, operating facility, and the mural can be viewed by interested members of the public. It resides on the wall in the lobby above the superintendent's door.

WEB: https://www.postofficefans.com/nutley-new-jersey-post-office/

Paulsboro

ADDRESS: 1015 N. Delaware St., Paulsboro, New Jersey 08066

ARTIST: Nena de Brennecke

TITLE: *Oil Refining*

MEDIUM: Wood (reliefs)

STATUS: The Paulsboro post office is still an active, operating facility, and the reliefs can be viewed by interested members of the public. They reside in the lobby on the wall above the postmaster's door.

WEB: https://www.postofficefans.com/paulsboro-new-jersey-post-office/

Penns Grove

ADDRESS: 56 W. Main St., Penns Grove, New Jersey 08069

ARTIST: Benjamin Hawkins

TITLE: *Early Traders*

MEDIUM: Stone (relief)

STATUS: The Penns Grove post office is still an active, operating facility, and the relief can be viewed by interested members of the public. It resides in the lobby on the wall above the retail entrance door.

WEB: https://www.postofficefans.com/penns-grove-new-jersey-post-office/

Pitman

ADDRESS: 55 N. Broadway, Pitman, New Jersey 08071

ARTIST: Nathaniel Choate

TITLE: *The Four Winds*

MEDIUM: Plaster (relief)

STATUS: The Pitman post office is still an active, operating facility, and the relief can be viewed by interested members of the public. It resides in the lobby on the wall above the postmaster's door.

WEB: https://www.postofficefans.com/pitman-new-jersey-post-office/

Plainfield

ADDRESS: 201 Watchung Ave., Plainfield, New Jersey 07060

ARTIST: Anton Refregier

TITLE: *Figures from American Folklore* and *Quilting Bee*

MEDIUM: Tempera (murals) 2 panels

STATUS: The Plainfield post office is still an active, operating facility, and the murals can be viewed by interested members of the public. One resides at the east end of the lobby, and one resides on the west end of the lobby.

WEB: https://www.postofficefans.com/plainfield-new-jersey-post-office/

Pompton Lakes

ADDRESS: 47 Lakeside Ave., Pompton Lakes, New Jersey 07442

ARTIST: Alexander Stirling Calder

TITLE: *Benjamin Franklin*

MEDIUM: Stone (relief)

STATUS: The Pompton Lakes post office is still an active, operating facility, and the relief can be viewed by interested members of the public. It resides in the lobby on the wall above the postmaster's door.

WEB: https://www.postofficefans.com/pompton-lakes-new-jersey-post-office/

Princeton

ADDRESS: 20 Palmer Square E., Princeton, New Jersey 08542

ARTIST: Karl Free

TITLE: *Columbia Under the Palm*

MEDIUM: Oil and tempera (mural)

STATUS: The Princeton post office is no longer an active, operating facility. The building is now privately owned, restricting access to the public. However, the mural is reported to still reside here, in the former post office lobby, on the wall above what was once the postmaster's door.

WEB: https://www.postofficefans.com/former-princeton-new-jersey-post-office/

Ridgefield Park

ADDRESS: 155 Main St., Ridgefield Park, New Jersey 07660

ARTIST: Thomas Donnelly

TITLE: *Washington Bridge*

MEDIUM: Oil on canvas (mural)

STATUS: The Ridgefield Park post office is still an active, operating facility, and the mural can be viewed by interested members of the public. It resides in the lobby on the wall above the postmaster's door.

WEB: https://www.postofficefans.com/ridgefield-park-new-jersey-post-office/

Ridgewood

ADDRESS: 143 E. Ridgewood Ave., Ridgewood, New Jersey 07450

ARTIST: Romuald Kraus

TITLE: *Two male and female figures*

MEDIUM: Metal (reliefs)

STATUS: The Ridgewood post office is still an active, operating facility, and the reliefs can be viewed by interested members of the public. They reside in the lobby on the wall above the retail counter. In addition there is a life-size sculpture of a mail carrier near the large tree in front of the building.

WEB: https://www.postofficefans.com/ridgewood-new-jersey-post-office/

RIVERSIDE

ADDRESS: 4 W. Scott St., Riverside, New Jersey 08075

ARTIST: John Poehler

TITLE: *The Town of Progress—1855*

MEDIUM: Oil on canvas (mural)

STATUS: The Riverside post office is still an active, operating facility, and the mural can be viewed by interested members of the public. It resides on a wall in the main lobby.

WEB: https://www.postofficefans.com/riverside-new-jersey-post-office/

Short Hills

ADDRESS: 30 Chatham Rd., Short Hills, New Jersey 07078

ARTIST: Ernest Lawson

TITLE: *Short Hills Landscape*

MEDIUM: Oil on canvas (mural)

STATUS: The Short Hills post office is still an active, operating facility. However, the mural has been reported missing, lost, or destroyed. It previously resided in the main lobby above the postmaster's door.

WEB: https://www.postofficefans.com/short-hills-new-jersey-post-office/

South Orange

ADDRESS: 31 Vose Ave., South Orange, New Jersey 07079

ARTIST: Bernard Perlin

TITLE: *Family Scene*

MEDIUM: Oil on canvas (mural)

STATUS: The South Orange post office is still an active, operating facility, and the mural can be viewed by interested members of the public. It resides in the lobby on the wall above the postmaster's door.

WEB: https://www.postofficefans.com/south-orange-new-jersey-post-office/

South River

ADDRESS: 44 Obert St., South River, New Jersey 08882

ARTIST: Maurice Glickman

TITLE: *Construction*

MEDIUM: Wood (relief)

STATUS: The South River post office is still an active, operating facility, and the relief can be viewed by interested members of the public. It resides in the lobby on the wall above the postmaster's door.

WEB: https://www.postofficefans.com/south-river-new-jersey-post-office/

Summit

ADDRESS: 61 Maple St., Summit, New Jersey 07901

ARTIST: Fiske Boyd

TITLE: *Arrival of First Train* and *Stage Coach Attack*

MEDIUM: Oil on canvas (murals)

STATUS: The Summit post office is still an active, operating facility. However, the murals have been reported missing, lost, or destroyed. They previously resided on the walls of the main lobby.

WEB: https://www.postofficefans.com/summit-new-jersey-post-office/

Toms River

ADDRESS: 40 Washington St., Toms River, New Jersey 08753

ARTIST: Milton Hebald

TITLE: *Boating on Barnegat Bay*

MEDIUM: Unknown (sculpture)

STATUS: The former Toms River post office is no longer an active, operating facility. The building is now home to O.C.E.A.N., Inc. The sculpture has been reported missing, lost, or destroyed. It previously resided in the lobby on the wall above the postmaster's door.

WEB: https://www.postofficefans.com/former-toms-river-new-jersey-post-office/

TRENTON

ADDRESS: 402 E. State St., Trenton, New Jersey 08608

ARTIST: Charles W. Ward

TITLE: *Second Battle of Trenton*, *Rural Delivery*, and *Glass Manufacture*

MEDIUM: Oil on canvas (murals)

STATUS: The former Trenton Post Office and Federal Building is still an active, operating federal building; however, the postal service no longer operates out of this facility. The murals can be viewed by interested members of the public. They reside on the walls of the main lobby. However, as of this writing, photography is prohibited.

WEB: https://www.postofficefans.com/trenton-new-jersey-post-office-courthouse/

Washington

ADDRESS: 36 Belvidere Ave., Washington, New Jersey 07882

ARTIST: Frank D. Shapiro

TITLE: *A Raising in Early New Jersey*

MEDIUM: Oil on canvas (mural)

STATUS: The Washington post office is still an active, operating facility, and the mural can be viewed by interested members of the public. It resides in the lobby on the wall above the postmaster's door.

WEB: https://www.postofficefans.com/washington-new-jersey-post-office/

West New York

ADDRESS: 5415 Bergenline Ave., West New York, New Jersey 07093

ARTIST: William Dean Fausett

TITLE: *View From the Palisades—West New York 1939*

MEDIUM: Oil on plywood (mural)

STATUS: The West New York post office is still an active, operating facility, and the mural can be viewed by interested members of the public. It resides in the lobby on the wall above the retail counter.

WEB: https://www.postofficefans.com/west-new-york-new-jersey-post-office/

Westfield

ADDRESS: 153 Central Ave., Westfield, New Jersey 07090

ARTIST: Roy Hilton

TITLE: *The New Stagecoach* and *Building of Westfield*

MEDIUM: Oil on canvas (murals)

STATUS: The Westfield post office is still an active, operating facility, and *The New Stagecoach* mural can be viewed by interested members of the public. It resides in the lobby on the wall above the postmaster's door. It is best viewed during business hours, as it is behind a glass window retail section. The second mural, *Building of Westfield*, has been reported, missing, lost, or destroyed.

WEB: https://www.postofficefans.com/westfield-new-jersey-post-office/

Westwood

ADDRESS: 216 Westwood Ave., Westwood, New Jersey 07675

ARTIST: Hunt Diederich

TITLE: *Pegasus with Messenger*

MEDIUM: Plaster (relief)

STATUS: The Westwood post office is still an active, operating facility. However, it has been reported the relief is missing, lost, or destroyed. It previously resided in the lobby on the wall above the postmaster's door.

WEB: https://www.postofficefans.com/westwood-new-jersey-post-office/

WILDWOOD

ADDRESS: 3311 Atlantic Ave., Wildwood, New Jersey 08260

ARTIST: Dennis Burlingame

TITLE: *Activities of the Fishing Fleet*

MEDIUM: Oil on canvas (murals) 2 panels

STATUS: The Wildwood post office is still an active, operating facility, and the murals can be viewed by interested members of the public. One mural resides in the retail section on the wall above the postmaster's door and is best viewed during business hours. The second mural resides on a wall in the main lobby.

WEB: https://www.postofficefans.com/wildwood-new-jersey-post-office/

Summary

I CREATED THIS BOOK as a reference for myself, as well as for those who are interested in these wonderful buildings and works of art. My goal is to provide you a valuable reference list of the buildings in New Jersey that house murals. For more information about each one and to participate in the discussion of any of the buildings or art, please visit www.postofficefans.com.

This book contains all the post offices in New Jersey that had art installed as a part of the New Deal. This book provides notes on the location, status, and accessibility of the art. I've personally visited and photographed each building and mural. Please note this is not a complete list of all the post office buildings constructed in New Jersey during the New Deal, only the ones that housed art.

I welcome your comments, suggestions, or feedback. You may reach me through the following social channels. Of course, I also welcome mail through the United States Postal Service, C/O Post Office Fans, PO Box 11, Crystal Lake, IL 60039.

About the Author

DAVID W. GATES JR. is a post office enthusiast and award-winning author who has traveled thousands of miles nationwide in search of historic post office buildings and art. He blogs about his work at:

www.postofficefans.com

Although the murals have been around for more than 86 years, David discovered how often these are overlooked. Join David in his quest to visit them all.

He lives in Crystal Lake, IL with his wife and son. When not photographing and documenting post offices, he can be found cooking, baking, hiking, or involved in do-it-yourself projects at home, not necessarily all at once and not necessarily in that order.

Other Titles by the Publisher

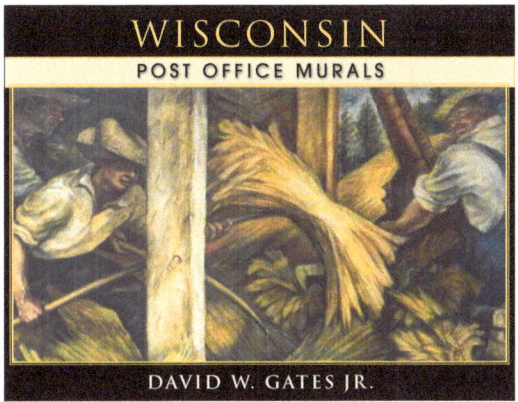

Wisconsin Post Office Murals

by David W. Gates Jr.

ISBN: 978-1-970088-00-7 (Paperback)
ISBN: 978-1-970088-01-4 (EPUB)
ISBN: 978-1-970088-02-1 (PDF)

Wisconsin Post Office Mural Guidebook

by David W. Gates Jr.

ISBN: 978-1-970088-09-0 (Paperback)

ISBN: 978-1-970088-10-6 (EPUB)
ISBN: 978-1-970088-11-3 (PDF)

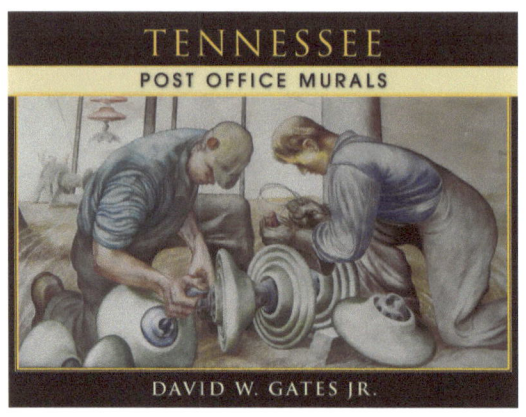

Tennessee Post Office Murals

by David W. Gates Jr.

ISBN: 978-1-970088-03-8 (Paperback)
ISBN: 978-1-970088-04-5 (EPUB)
ISBN: 978-1-970088-05-2 (PDF)

Tennessee Post Office Mural Guidebook

by David W. Gates Jr.

ISBN: 978-1-970088-0-69 (Paperback)
ISBN: 978-1-970088-0-76 (EPUB)
ISBN: 978-1-970088-0-83 (PDF)

Illinois Post Office Mural Guidebook

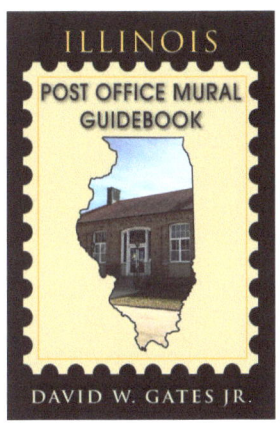

by David W. Gates Jr.

ISBN: 978-1-970088-12-0 (Paperback)
ISBN: 978-1-970088-13-7 (EPUB)
ISBN: 978-1-970088-14-4 (PDF)

www.ingramcontent.com/pod-product-compliance
Lightning Source LLC
Chambersburg PA
CBHW041215070526
44579CB00006B/61